Well Made, Fair Trade

My BED
and other home furniture

Helen Greathead

W
FRANKLIN WATTS
LONDON · SYDNEY

D1379984

Franklin Watts
Published in 2017 by the Watts Publishing Group

Copyright © Franklin Watts 2015

All rights reserved.

Series Editor: Julia Bird
Packaged by: Q2A Media

ISBN 978 1 4451 3283 9

Printed in China

Franklin Watts
An imprint of
Hachette Children's Group
Part of The Watts Publishing Group
Carmelite House
50 Victoria Embankment
London EC4Y 0DZ

An Hachette UK Company
www.hachette.co.uk

www.franklinwatts.co.uk

MIX
Paper from
responsible sources
FSC® C104740

Front Cover: Pinkcandy, Ewa Studio, Robert_s, Chen ws, Holbox, Graphixmania/Shutterstock. Back Cover: Iriana Shiyan/Shutterstock. Title Page: Baker Alhashki, Ksenia Palimski, PzAxe, Graphixmania, Chukcha, Getideaka, Viphotos, Ozaiachin/Shutterstock. Imprint Page: Syda Productions/Shutterstock. P4: Semarang Suite; P5(T): Leonid Ikan/Shutterstock, P5(B): Ekler/Shutterstock; P6–7(BKGRD): K. Miri Photography/Shutterstock, P6: K. Miri Photography/Shutterstock; P7(T): TongChuwit/Shutterstock, P7(BR): Sasimoto/Shutterstock, P7(BL): David Selman/Cardinal/Corbis; P8–9(BKGRD): K. Miri Photography/Shutterstock, P8(B): White Lotus, P8(T): Frank Polich/Reuters; P9(B): Leslye Davis/The New York Times/Redux Pictures; P10–11(BKGRD): Ti Santi/Shutterstock, P10(B): Monkey Business Images/Shutterstock; P11(B): Thor Jorgen Udvang/Shutterstock, P11(T): Andrew Rowat/ Getty Images; P12: Lou Linwei/Alamy, P12–13(BKGRD): Ti Santi/Shutterstock, P13(T): Kisno Weaver (INORI)/ Fairtrade Furniture, P13(B): Ruzpage/Shutterstock; P14–15(BKGRD): Tom Gowanlock/Shutterstock, P14(B): Nikolpetr/Shutterstock; P15(T): D 200 Collection/Balan Madhavan/Alamy, P15(C): FLPA /Alamy, P15(B): Picsfive/ Shutterstock; P16(L): Picsfive/Shutterstock, P16(BR): Fabien Monteil/Shutterstock, P16(TR):Studio Swine; P17(T): Tom Gowanlock/Shutterstock, P17(B): Anna Beruad/Malika org; P18: wavebreakmedia/Shutterstock; P19(B): Hector Conesa/Shutterstock, P19(T): Lisette Van Der Hoorn/Shutterstock; P20(T):Forest Stewardship Council, P20(B): Guentermanaus/Shutterstock; P21(T): TongChuwit/Shutterstock, P21(C): Siiren, P21(B): Sneh Gupta 2014; P22-23(BKGRD): Fredredhat/Shutterstock, P22(CL):IlyaAkinshin/Shutterstock, P22(CR):Ilya Akinshin/Shutterstock, P22(C): Andresr/Shutterstock; P23(C): Alan Bailey/Shutterstock, P23(T):Ilya Akinshin/Shutterstock; P24(TL):Ilya Akinshin/Shutterstock, P24(TR): TongChuwit/Shutterstock, P24(B): Sue Smith/Shutterstock, P24(C): Ross Parry Picture Agency; P25(T): Akintunde Akinleye/Reuters, P25(B): Friedrich Stark/Alamy, P26(CR): FedeCandoniPhoto/ Shutterstock, P26(CL):Ahmad Faizal Yahya/Shutterstock, P26–27(BKGRD): Maffi/Shutterstock, P27(BL):Ten Thousand Villages, P27(BC):Ten Thousand Villages, P27(T): Goodweave.org, P27(BR):Ahmad Faizal Yahya/ Shutterstock; P28–29(BKGRD): Maffi/Shutterstock, P28(T): Goodweave.org, P28(B): Goodweave.org; P29(BR): Designboom, P29(BL): MadeByNode; P30–31: Andresr, Fabien Monteil, Hector Conesa, Monkey Business Images, Ruzpage; Ahmad Faizal Yahya, Nikolpetr,FedeCandoniPhoto,Leonid Ikan, Wavebreakmedia, K. Miri Photography/ Shutterstock; D 200 Collection/Balan Madhavan/Alamy; Semarang suite; Kisno weaver (INORI)/Fairtrade Furniture; Lou Linwei/Alamy; P32(T): Fabien Monteil/Shutterstock. Illustrations: all-free-downloads.com: (4–5, 18–19, 19–20)

Contents

Words in **bold** can be found in the glossary on page 30.

Fair trade furniture

Furniture is big business. Today, many companies are starting to look at how furniture can be made in a way that is fair to workers and safe for the environment.

Why buy fair trade?

Around the world many problems are caused through furniture production. Workers may be badly paid and suffer poor working conditions, or face danger from the chemicals they use in glue or paint. The World Fair Trade Organisation (WFTO) is an international group of companies that believe in fair trade practice. Companies who belong to the WFTO pay their workers fairly, help to care for local **communities** and make sure that nothing they do damages wildlife or the environment.

The Fair Trade Furniture Company is a member of the WFTO. Its furniture is made in Indonesia using natural materials. The company's workers are paid a fair wage and have health and education programmes.

What is best to buy?

When buying new furniture it is important to know what it is made of and where it has come from. This is known as the **supply chain**. When your family is buying a new item of furniture, look carefully at any labels or logos. Does it have a WFTO label or a Forest Stewardship Council (FSC) logo? The FSC is a US company that makes sure that trees used to make furniture have come from forests that are well-managed and **sustainable** (see page 20).

The FSC looks after the future of the world's forests and protects the well-being of local communities and wildlife.

What can I do?

This book will explain how fair trade schemes help workers to make a decent living, improve working conditions and also protect the environment and wildlife. It will give you ideas about what you can do to help when choosing furniture with your family and how to recycle old or unwanted furniture.

This map shows the places mentioned in the book that are involved in fair trade projects.

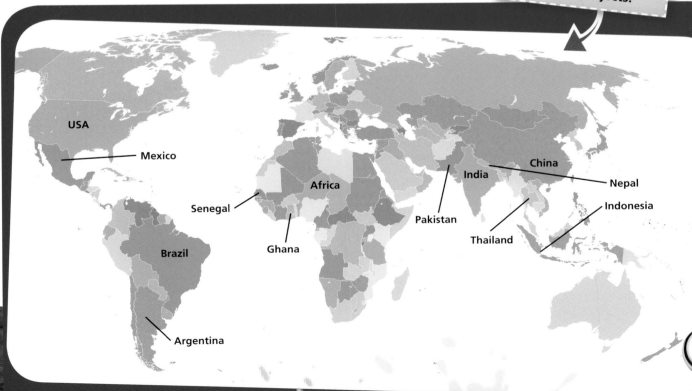

USA
Mexico
China
India
Nepal
Africa
Senegal
Indonesia
Pakistan
Ghana
Thailand
Brazil
Argentina

Beds and mattresses

The first mattresses were made of straw, leaves and even animal skins. Today, mattresses contain many different parts.

How are mattresses made?

Mattresses with springs were first made in the mid-18th century. Today, the inside of a sprung mattress is made up of 250 to 1,000 connecting springs, with from five to eight layers of cushioning around them. Some parts of the mattress are made up by hand, but the quilted fabric cover is stitched using a giant quilting machine, then cut to size and added to the mattress.

The quilted padding that covers the top, bottom and sides of most mattresses is machine made in factories

Where are beds and mattresses made?

Beds and mattresses are manufactured all over the world, with China and the USA being the main producers. China and Poland **export** more mattresses than any other country. The Sealy Mattress Company is the world's largest manufacturer of beds and mattresses. The main company is based in Ohio, USA, but it is represented in many other countries, including Saudi Arabia, Japan, Australia and Argentina.

Many bed and mattress companies source their materials from around the world. For example, the Turkish company, Boycelik, manufactures mattress springs made from carbon steel wire, and sources the wire rods for the springs in Europe and Turkey. It exports the finished springs to 65 countries around the world.

Re-use, recycle

Today, 90 per cent of beds and mattresses can be recycled. Metal from the mattress springs can be melted down and re-used; wooden bed frames may be broken up and used for garden **mulch**; paper, plastic and fabrics can be used for building **insulation**.

Getting rid of old mattresses can be a problem. Millions used to end up in **landfill** sites.

Some mattresses have springs inside to help keep them firm, but which also allow them to move when we move.

Health risks

Mattresses and cushions are often treated with **toxic** glues and **flame-retardants**. These coatings can damage the health of the people who make mattresses and cushions, because they inhale toxic fumes that can make them ill. Workers need proper protection from glue and other sprays and should work in spaces that are well **ventilated**.

Sleep safe

Sometimes flame retardants are mixed with the foam that is produced for use in mattresses. Sleeping on these foam mattresses can cause an allergic reaction, such as swollen eyes or lips, rashes and difficulty breathing. Natural **latex** is a safe alternative.

This mattress is being tested to see if it contains enough flame retardant. In the USA, the law says a mattress has to be able to withstand a two-foot (60 cm) wide blowtorch flame for 70 seconds.

Best buy!

White Lotus produce mattresses in New Jersey, USA, using natural materials and no chemicals. Instead of springs, the core of the mattress is made from natural latex, a plant-based material that is **biodegradable**. White Lotus mattresses do not need to be treated with dangerous flame-retardants, as the outer layer of organic wool padding is naturally flame-proof.

The **latex** core of this White Lotus mattress is wrapped in 100 per cent New Zealand wool and 100 per cent organic cotton.

Case study: Taylorsville furniture factory, North Carolina, USA

In 2010, Sheri Farley was working in a furniture factory in Taylorsville, North Carolina, USA. Factory workers were paid US $9 (£5.39) an hour, to glue **polyurethane** foam to chairs, sofas and mattresses. The work involved standing all day and using a spray gun to apply the glue. The pay was reasonable, but it hardly made up for the illness Sheri went on to suffer.

Better place to work

Sheri stayed at the factory for five years, but today she is no longer well enough to work. It is likely that a chemical (n-propyl bromide, or nPB) in the glue damaged nerve endings in Sheri's body, causing severe pain along her spine and in her legs. One in seven people suffers after working with the glue, and the effects can show up in just two weeks. Facemasks and proper ventilation in the workplace could have solved the problem.

Following US government research and tests carried out on the glue, it was given a hazard warning in 2013. Employers are now expected to:
- limit the amount of time employees spend using the glue in the workplace
- provide breathing masks and clothing for their staff
- train employees to use the glue safely.

Sheri Farley walks with a limp and uses a stick for support. She finds it difficult to balance and is frequently in pain.

Armchairs and sofas

Your sofa is probably one of the most expensive pieces of furniture in your home. That is because it took time, care and specialist knowledge to make.

How are sofas and chairs made?

It can take up to 600 hours to make a top-quality sofa and most of the work has to be done by hand. First, the wooden frame is built, then strips of **webbing** are added to hold the seat in place. Springs may be attached to the webbing with **twine**. The padding, which is added to each section separately, might be made from horsehair, foam or **polyester**. It is sewn into place and held in position with fabric coverings. The panels for the outer cover are cut, stapled or sewn on, then cushions are added.

Soft armchairs and sofas can contain up to 1,000 tacks, 180 metres of twine and hundreds of metres of sewing thread.

Where are sofas and chairs made?

Traditionally, Italy was the top producer of quality leather sofas. In 1998, one Italian company started producing its sofas in China. The Chinese workers were paid less and worked longer hours so furniture made in China was much cheaper to produce. Many US companies moved their factories to China, too. Lots of different sorts of chairs and sofas began to be made here, as well as various other kinds of furniture.

Workers in a furniture factory in China cut and style leather and fur material to cover chairs and sofas.

Low pay, long hours

Working in Chinese furniture factories can be tough, with long hours and low pay. Factories may be overcrowded and unsafe, with workers offered little protection from cutting equipment or paint and varnish fumes. Young Chinese people today are better educated than their parents and want better opportunities, as a result, factory employers are starting to offer salaries above the minimum wage and improved conditions.

Spraying varnish on furniture in a production line in a factory in China.

Case study: China's furniture factories

In 2005, 300,000 furniture jobs were lost in the US and moved to China. Whilst US workers could earn over $15 an hour, in 2008 the same jobs in China paid just 70 cents an hour. In 2008, twenty-five year old Zhao Xia worked in a factory preparing furniture for painting. She had only two days off each month and regularly worked until midnight. She lived with her husband in a small room near the factory. Zhao Xia put up with these conditions, rather than work in the fields all day. Today, workers' attitudes have begun to change.

Factory workers sewing upholstery for furniture in Guanddong, southern China.

Better place to work

Circle Furniture, based in Shenzhen, China, manufactures living room suites and a wide range of other furniture. The owner of the company, Bruce Lee, understands that in order to keep good workers he has to be a fair employer. The company now provides food and accommodation where workers can live with their families. Some workers are even given a free motor scooter to use for their journey to and from the factory. With young workers increasingly unhappy about factory pay and working conditions, perhaps more employers will follow Circle Furniture's example in the future.

Renewable rattan

Rattan looks like bamboo and grows in areas with tropical rainforests, such as Indonesia. It has become popular for use in fair trade furniture because it is easier to cut down and transport than **timber**, and it grows back much faster. It is also light, tough and flexible the perfect sustainable material.

Best buy!

Inori is an agency that helps small producers of traditionally made Indonesian chairs find fair trade buyers. They work with Kisno, a small family workshop, and Mandiri Craft, which trains disabled people to make seat frames and other wooden furniture parts. Mandiri Craft employs up to 50 workers who might otherwise have no work because of their disabilities.

Kisno furniture is woven by hand following local Indonesian skills and traditions.

About 80 per cent of the world's raw rattan products come from Indonesia. Rattan is bendy so can be woven to make furniture as well as pots and baskets.

Plastic furniture

Plastic furniture is cheap, lightweight and useful. However, making and disposing of it is having a negative impact on the environment.

How is plastic furniture made?

Plastic furniture was first introduced at the end of the 1940s because of a demand for low-cost home furnishings. Today, the cheapest plastic furniture is made using injection moulding. This process involves a shaped metal mould that is filled with **polypropylene** that has been heated to a specific temperature. The mould cools down and a solid plastic piece of furniture is removed. This is called monobloc furniture because it is made in one piece, with no need for joins.

Due to **mass production**, plastic chairs and tables are very cheap and are now seen everywhere. Plastic furniture is especially popular for use outdoors in gardens.

Mass production

Today, mass production can turn out hundreds of thousands of monobloc chairs each year. At first, production was limited to France and the US, but now the chairs are made in Russia, Taiwan, Australia, Mexico, USA, Europe, Turkey, Israel and China. It is estimated that one monobloc chair is made every minute.

This factory in India produces plastic furniture, including monobloc chairs.

What is wrong with plastic?

Plastic is made from oil and gas – **fossil fuels** that aren't renewable. Making plastic furniture uses up to four per cent of all the oil and gas that is produced each year, and a further three to four per cent is used to manufacture the furniture itself. Plastic furniture may be light and easy to use, but it also takes thousands of years to break down. In Europe, 50 per cent of our plastic waste, including furniture, still goes to landfill.

Plastic chairs, such as this red one, are cheap to buy so people often don't think twice about throwing them away. Millions end up on rubbish dumps or in landfill.

Floating on the ocean

An estimated 100,000 tonnes of plastic waste, such as bags, bottles and even furniture, has made its way into the sea. The plastic breaks down into smaller microplastics, which are easily swallowed. Many animals and birds are killed or injured as a result. Chemical additives from the plastics can also get into the **food chain** through fish that are eaten by humans and animals.

Responsible waste

Plastic furniture doesn't have to go to waste. It can easily be recycled by businesses and individual consumers through local recycling schemes. In the USA in 2012, over 1,800 companies specialised in the disposal of all types of plastic waste, but only nine per cent of discarded plastics were disposed of responsibly.

Best buy!

An 'island' of plastic twice the size of the USA floats on the Pacific Ocean, and it's getting bigger. This stool, from the Sea Chair Project, was made by design students who are worried about sea pollution. The chair is made entirely from plastic reclaimed from the sea.

Each item made for the Sea Chair Project has a tag with its production number and other data to show where the plastic came from.

Every year, thousands of tonnes of plastic rubbish are washed up on beaches around the world. This causes pollution and danger to people and wildlife.

Case study: recycled plastics, Senegal, West Africa

In Senegal, West Africa, plastic pollution in the city of Thiès was so bad that the local people approached an Italian waste management organisation for help. By 2002, their region had two plastic recycling centres. Today, plastic is brought to the centres (sometimes by donkey and cart) to be sorted into colour and type and then washed. Creating enough heat to melt the plastic uses too much electricity and causes carbon dioxide **emissions** that damage the atmosphere, so here plastic is cut into small pieces by hand and then ground into pellets or powders by machine.

Jobs and training

The centres create jobs for local people and provide training in management, accountancy and how to operate machines. Adults can also learn how to read and write here. By 2008, one centre had recycled 150 tonnes of plastic, and prevented an estimated 273 tonnes of carbon dioxide emissions.

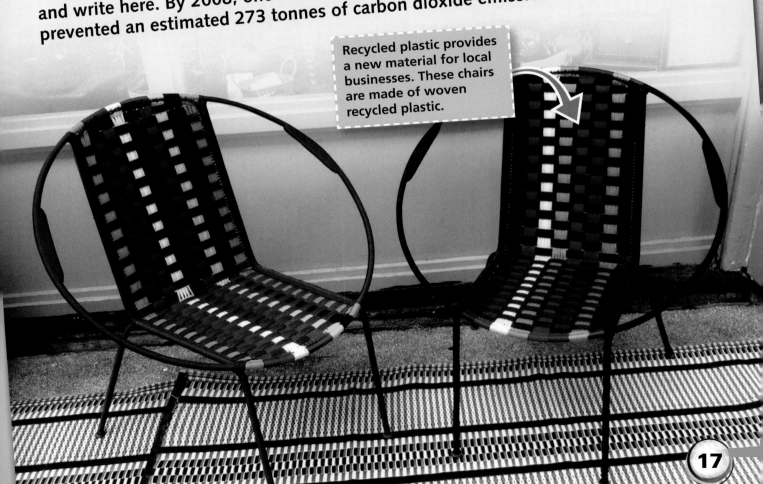

Recycled plastic provides a new material for local businesses. These chairs are made of woven recycled plastic.

Wooden furniture

The demand for furniture made from wood is growing and this is causing problems as forests are being destroyed around the world.

A wooden table is hardwearing, but the wood may not have come from a sustainable forest.

How are tables made?

Tables have been used for centuries. Today, most are made from wood and held together with glue and screws. Planks of wood are stored at 10–29°C, so the wood does not shrink or expand. The planks are glued to make the tabletop, and clamped together while the glue dries. Then the top is sanded down and cut to shape. The legs are shaped on a machine called a profiler. The table is assembled and stained, then sealed, sanded and **lacquered** by hand.

Where does the wood come from?

Some wood for furniture comes from tropical rainforests, while other types come from sustainable forests that are grown specifically for use in making furniture. Asian countries, such as China, India, Vietnam, Indonesia and Malaysia, produce a huge amount of timber. India has some of the largest rainforests in the world, and 93 per cent of its furniture exports are made from wood.

Large areas of rainforest are disappearing every day through **logging** and forest clearance to produce timber for furniture. The loss of rainforest has a devastating effect on the environment and on local people.

Millions of trees are cut down and turned into logs to be made into furniture. This means rainforests around the world are shrinking.

In Cameroon, West Africa, the Baka people use rainforest trees and plants for vital medicines. But in south-east Cameroon, nearly all Baka land has been lost to loggers.

Global warming

When the rainforest is cut down, the land dries out very quickly because it is no longer sheltered from the Sun. Plants and wildlife that live in the forest die, too. Trees absorb carbon dioxide from the atmosphere, so fewer trees means more carbon dioxide emissions in the atmosphere, which increases **global warming**.

Deforestation in the Amazon, the world's biggest tropical rainforest. Over 440 new species of animals and plants have been discovered over the past four years in this vast forest. But it is estimated 150 acres of rainforest around the world are burnt every minute.

Sustaining the forests

At the current rate of **deforestation**, it is estimated that in 100 years there will be no rainforests left. However, with proper control and management, wood can be produced sustainably. Many organisations, such as the Forest Stewardship Council, have schemes around the world that ensure proper management of forests, bringing opportunities for fair employment and maintaining and protecting the wildlife habitats.

Look for the FSC logo on wood or paper items you buy.

Special policy

Kingfisher is Europe's largest home improvement company with over 1,000 stores in nine countries. A third of Kingfisher's products are made from timber. Eighty-nine per cent of the wood they use is sustainable, but by 2020 Kingfisher aims to increase this figure to 100 per cent. To improve sustainability they are starting to enlarge some of the forests in the countries where the company is based. By 2050, they hope to create more forest than they need to use, leaving the unused forest as a habitat for wildlife.

Case study: Myakka fair trade company

All furniture produced by Myakka, a UK company, is fair trade, and made in India, Indonesia and Thailand. The company uses sustainable **hardwoods** from **certified suppliers** and helps fund replanting schemes in Indonesia. Buying directly from the furniture manufacturer keeps Myakka's supply chain short, and payment to the producers high. They pay a fair price, which means better conditions for workers, and benefits for their families, too. One small producer has now bought the land its workshops are built on.

School for disabled children

Myakka also supports a boarding school for disabled children in Rajasthan, India. Here over 500 disabled children learn skills that will help them to find work. Donations from Myakka support the school's career training centre, where some of Myakka's products are made.

This brightly coloured table by Budi uses recycled wood.

Re-use, recycle

This table is made from recycled wooden Indonesian fishing boats. Bali artist Budi sells all his furniture through a fair trade exporter called Siiren. He gets a fair price for his work and Siiren makes sure that all their craftsmen benefit from good working conditions.

Raj Kanwar lost the use of her legs at the age of two. The training she receives at the boarding school gives her hope that, despite her disability, she will have the skills to find work in the future.

Refrigerators

Fridges enable people to keep food fresh for quite a while, but some of the chemicals fridges contain can cause serious damage to the environment if they are not disposed of properly.

The energy we waste keeping the fridge door open each year could run a dishwasher twenty times.

What are refrigerators made from?

The earliest fridges were holes in the ground, lined with straw or wood and packed with ice or snow. Today's refrigerators usually have a steel casing, with vacuum-formed plastic on the inside. The space between the inside and outside of the fridge is filled with foam, to keep the inner shell cool, whilst tubes filled with a cooling substance pass from a **condenser** at the bottom of the fridge, around the insides, keeping the contents 5°C or below, which slows the growth of bacteria in food.

Where are fridges made?

Jacob Perkins, of Massachusetts, USA, made the first working refrigeration machine in 1834. Fridges soon caught on and today refrigerators are produced all over the world. Many fridge factories in developing countries such as Brazil and India pay workers poorly for long working hours in unsafe conditions.

Case study: Whirlpool Corporation, Brazil

In Argentina, Brazil, India and Mexico the US company, Whirlpool Corporation, has been voted one of the best places to work. Whirlpool believes that employees must work in a healthy and safe environment; they must be treated with respect; they must be paid at least the minimum amount recommended by their local laws for all the hours they work, and they should not work more than 60 hours a week.

Whirlpool offers classes in workplace skills, such as computing.

Work for women

Whirlpool runs a variety of community projects, such as a scheme to improve employment opportunities for women in Brazil. The schemes help younger women who are single parents and may have difficulty finding work, as well as older women who may never have learned to read or write. Business **co-operatives** sponsored by the scheme provide workshops, classes and educational support, which help the women's employment prospects.

Getting rid of old fridges

Old fridges use up to three times the electricity of newer models, and they can contain now banned chemicals, called CFCs, which are dangerous to human health, and harmful to the **ozone layer**. Dumping old fridges can cause many problems. Discarded fridges from Europe are often shipped to developing countries such as Ghana, where they may be bought cheaply for use in the home, or dumped on illegal scrap heaps. Local people, including children, make money by taking the fridges apart and selling on any materials they can.

The chemicals in fridges and freezers can leak when fridges are dumped and can be dangerous to the local people and environment.

Re-use, recycle

This solar fridge works simply by using two cylinders, one inside the other. The space in between is filled with sand, wool or soil and soaked with water. In the heat of the Sun, the water evaporates, keeping the contents of the inner cylinder at a temperature of 6°C.

English schoolgirl Emily Cummins designed this fridge when she was just 16 years old. It is easy to make using scrap materials, such as leaky barrels or old car parts.

Sustainable fridges designed by Emily Cummins are now used in Zambia, Namibia and South Africa.

Case study: Agbogbloshie, Accra, Ghana

Agbogbloshie is a poor town and scrap heap on the outskirts of Ghana's capital city, Accra. Here, a group of scrap pickers take fridges apart, sell what they don't need and keep the metal. In their workshop, the metal is then cut and hammered into cooking pots, or 'head pans', which construction workers use for carrying concrete on their heads. The workers sell each pan for up to £2.35.

Banned shipments

Ghana banned shipments of second-hand fridges in January 2013 because of environmental concerns, but at the end of the year some were still arriving. The Ghanaian government now plans to offer discounts on new fridges to stop the trade in second-hand appliances, and hopes to create more and safer jobs by manufacturing them locally.

A 'head pan' being used on a construction site in Nigeria.

Young men in Ghana breaking up old refrigerators. One old fridge will make between eight and ten cooking pots.

25

Carpets and rugs

Carpets can be both beautiful and practical, whether they are made in a modern factory or produced by hand following age-old traditions.

Carpets are made all over the world, from the UK to China. Persian carpets (from Iran) are well known for their high quality, and date back 2,500 years.

How are carpets made?

To produce a **tufted** carpet, strips of yarn are spun together. The yarn is stitched onto backing material. Patterns and colours are added, the pieces of carpet are stitched together and the back is coated with latex. The carpet is steamed, brushed, vacuumed and trimmed before it is rolled into a tube, ready to go to the shops.

Child labour

In some parts of South Asia, children aged seven to fourteen are 'employed' to make rugs and carpets, often to pay off a family debt. The children receive very low pay, or become unpaid slaves in the industry. They work long hours in cramped, dark conditions with not enough food. Their eyesight, growth and breathing (through inhaling fine wool fibres) can all be affected. Sharp tools cause injuries, too.

GoodWeave was set up in 1994 by Kailash Satyarthi, an Indian children's **rights activist**. The group is made up of charities and non-profit organisations. It has been working to end illegal child labour in South Asia and inspects carpet factories, freeing child workers and helping them to get a proper education.

Carpets carrying the GoodWeave symbol show that they do not use child labour. Profits help to fund factory inspections and educate freed child workers.

Best buy!

Bunyaad is a group based around Lahore in Pakistan. It sells beautiful hand-crafted rugs in Canada and the USA. Bunyaad started work in the 1960s to help keep jobs and the age-old rug-making traditions alive in small villages. Today, Bunyaad works with about 850 families in 100 villages. The workers are paid a fair wage and extra fair trade income might buy a water buffalo, for example, to provide yogurt and butter, essential to Pakistani cooking.

These all-wool rugs made by workers from Bunyaad are hand-spun, using only natural dyes. They take 10 to 12 months to make.

Case study: Kathmandu, Nepal

Sanju lives in Kathmandu and is one of tens of thousands of 'carpet kids' throughout South Asia. Aged 11, she was sent to work in a carpet factory by her family who could not afford to look after her. Young children are used to make carpets because their small fingers are good for knotting handmade carpets. Sanju didn't receive any payment, worked from 4 am until 8 pm, had no time off and was always hungry. She cried every day.

A better life

Sanju thought things would never change, but one day an inspector from GoodWeave visited the factory, and helped to get her and other children to their **rehabilitation** centre. Now Sanju goes to school and takes parts in sports, and lives back at home with her family. She is also helping to teach the other young girls that come to the centre.

In this painting Sanju has shown herself without arms (right) because she felt trapped and very unhappy. Then she appears on the left with her arms outspread to show how much she has grown now she feels free.

Thanks to the education provided by GoodWeave, Sanju now believes she has a much brighter future and is learning to enjoy herself and have fun.

Untouchables

Kumbeshwar Technical School (KTS) began as a project to help people in Nepal who were 'untouchable'. This means people who were the lowest in their **caste** or social system. Untouchables could only work in certain jobs, such as cleaning the streets and sewers, in exchange for scraps of food. The Kumbeshwar project began in 1983 with a childcare programme and a literacy course for adults. The adults were then trained in knitting and carpet weaving and, by 1985, they began selling their wares. By selling through fair trade organisations, such as Node, the project now also funds an orphanage and a primary school. In 2013, some Node rugs were even exhibited in London's Design Museum.

Best buy!

Node is a not-for-profit business that creates fair trade rugs using designs by illustrators and designers from around the world – you can even design your own! The carpets are made by hand, using pure Tibetan wool, dyed with natural dyes that do not harm the environment, and knotted onto **looms** by hand.

Node rug makers are founder members of Fair Trade Nepal. Workers receive fair wages and the company supports a school of 260 children, as well as an orphanage.

This suitcase used to be a carpet! Recycled carpets mixed with **resin** from rapeseed oil make up the case's hard shell.

Environment matters

Today, you can buy carpets with reduced or recycled yarn or recycled backing material. Installing carpets without glue, and using carpet tiles (so you only replace areas that are worn) also helps make new carpets more environmentally friendly. At the end of its life a carpet can be recycled.

Glossary

biodegradable a substance that can be broken down, e.g. by bacteria, without causing pollution

caste part of a class system in Hinduism

certified suppliers people in the supply chain who have been checked and approved to follow the regulations required

co-operative group of people, or organisations, working together and sharing any benefits or profits evenly between them

communities groups of people who live and work closely together

condenser series of copper tubes inside a fridge that help transfer heat from the inside of the fridge to the outside

deforestation cutting down of trees, especially when they are valuable to the environment

emissions the release or discharge of substances, such as gases

export to sell goods outside of the country where they were made

flame-retardant something, which stops an item of furniture catching fire

food chain the order in which food is eaten by living things, such as humans eating big fish that eat smaller fish

fossil fuels natural materials such as oil or coal which come from the Earth

global warming the gradual rise in the Earth's temperature caused by air pollution, from gases such as carbon dioxide

hardwoods wood from trees that produce seeds which are covered by some sort of fruit or shell

insulation material used as a protective layer

lacquered painted with a shiny finish

landfill site a place for dumping waste sometimes by burying it in the ground. In landfill rubbish decomposes very, very slowly

latex an artificial rubber-like material

logging chopping down trees and preparing them for sale

loom machine used for weaving

mass production making a huge amount of the same thing by machine

mulch a covering of rotting vegetable matter or leaves that is spread over soil to protect plants or help them to grow

ozone layer layer around the Earth's atmosphere that protects it from ultra-violet rays from the Sun

polyester a synthetic fabric

polyurethane a synthetic material used in paint and varnish

polypropylene a synthetic resin used as a moulding material

rattan a creeping plant that grows from the forest floor in tropical rainforests, using the trees to climb upwards

rehabilitation helping people to rebuild their life

resin a sticky liquid that oozes from some trees and plants

rights activist a person who goes on marches and is very active in fighting for the rights of other people, animals or the environment

supply chain the order of how materials or goods are put together to produce a finished product

sustainable when a resource can be used or grown again and again

timber when the wood from trees has been prepared and is ready to be made into products such as furniture

toxic poisonous or harmful

tufted where yarn for a carpet is inserted into a ready woven backing, which is then stuck to another backing material

twine a strong thread

ventilated has a supply of fresh air

webbing strong, narrow fabric used in chairs to make a base for chair seats

Websites

Visit the FAIRTRADE website to find out more about Fairtrade, and the products you can buy:
www.fairtrade.net
www.fairtrade.org.uk

Ask your local council about recycling possibilities, or find a charitable way to recycle them through the Furniture Reuse Network: **www.frn.org.uk**

Find out more about the Sea Chair Project, and the dangers of plastic waste in our oceans: **www.studioswine.com/seachair**

See what else can be done with an old fishing boat here: **www.siiren.co.uk/departments-c334/ethnic-rustic-furniture-c265/hand-carved-solid-wooden-recycled-boat-table-p1497**

See more of Emily Cummins' inventions here: **www.emilycummins.co.uk/about**

Read the stories of some of the children who have been freed from working in the carpet industry: **www.goodweave.org/about/children_stories**

See some fabulous Node rug designs and a video that shows how they are made here: **www.madebynode.com/**

Check out what the Fair Trade Furniture Company has to say about protecting the environment: **fairtradefurniture.co.uk/modern-conservatory-furniture/environment/**

Learn more about Ten Thousand Villages: **www.tenthousandvillages.ca/about** and for more on the people who work at Bunyaad see: **rugs.tenthousandvillages.com/people_behind_rugs**

There's lots more about managing forests at **www.fsc-uk.org**

Index